Finger Exercises for the Cello

Book One

by Cassia Harvey

CHP101

©2004 by C. Harvey Publications® All Rights Reserved.

www.charveypublications.com - print books

www.learnstrings.com - PDF downloadable books

Finger Exercises for the Cello

Book One

Practice Suggestions

1. Play with full bows and strong tone.

2. With the left hand, play on the tips of the fingers. Keep the fingers curved.

   Concentrate especially on the position of the 3rd and 4th fingers.

3. Press the strings down firmly and completely.

4. Take a short rest if your fingers get tired or if your hand hurts at all.

5. Start slowly. Only play faster when the notes are in tune.

6. Sit up straight and focus on good form.

4

Finger Exercises

1

Cassia Harvey

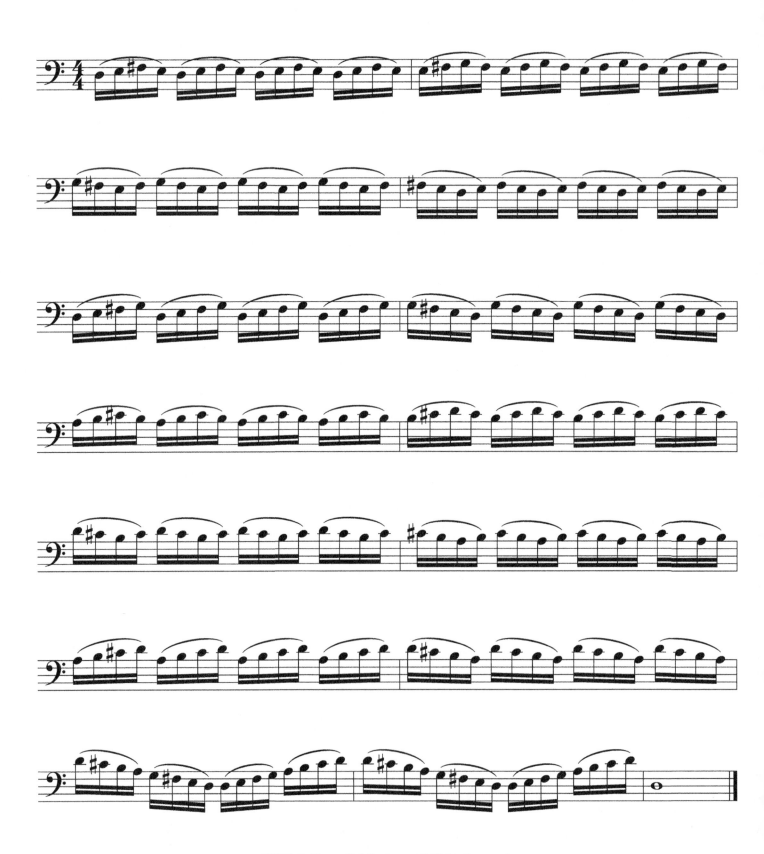

2

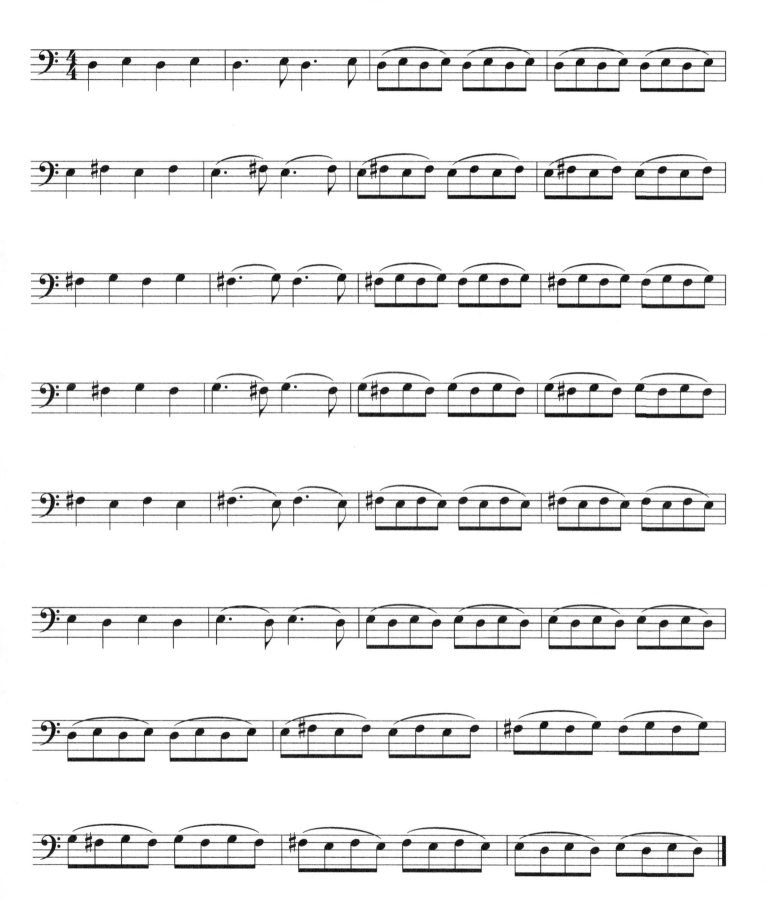

3

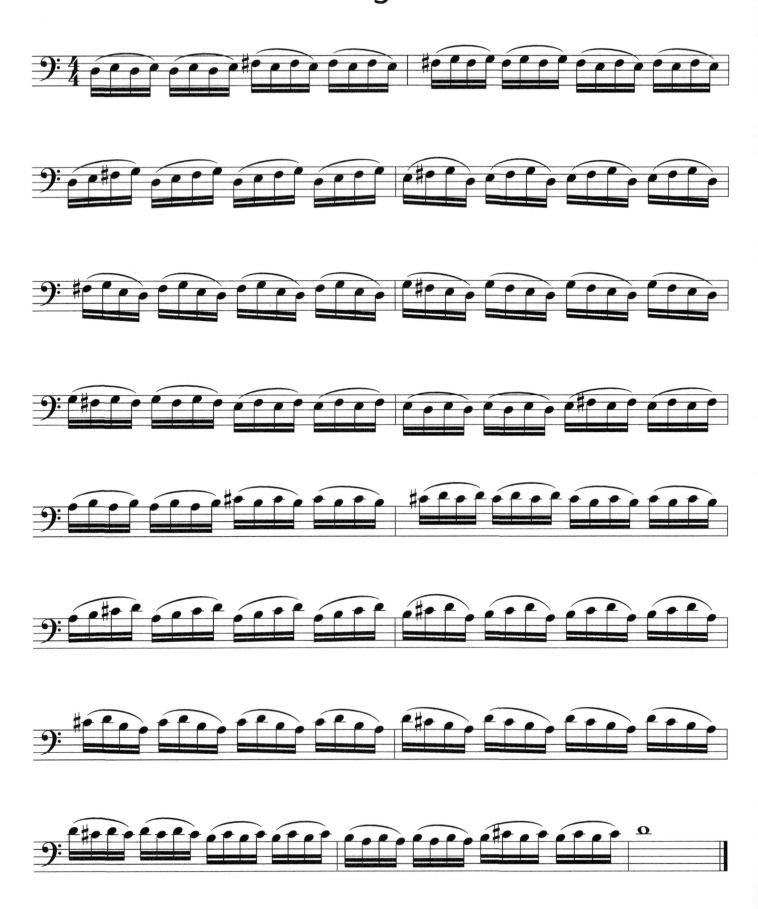

4

5

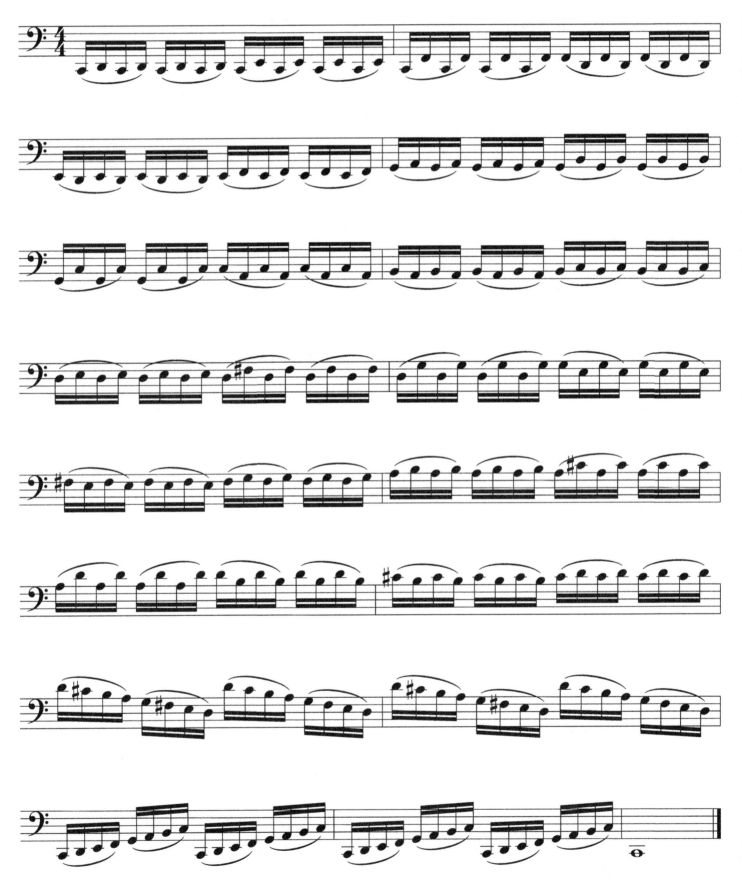

6

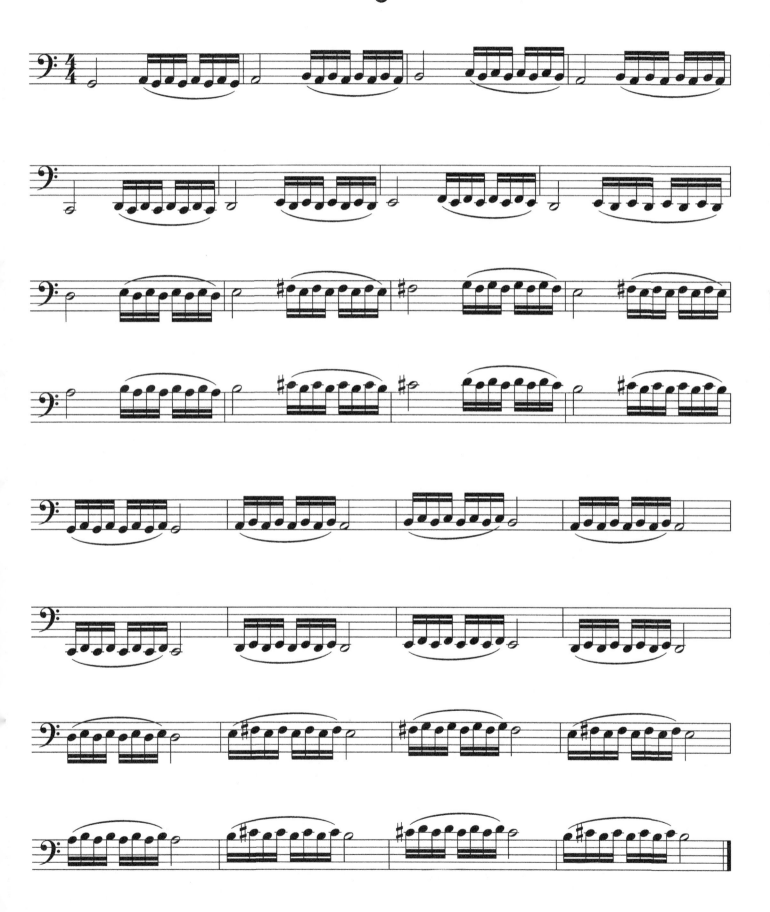

7

8

Separate bows

9

10

Separate bows.

Separate bows.

Separate bows.

Separate bows.

11

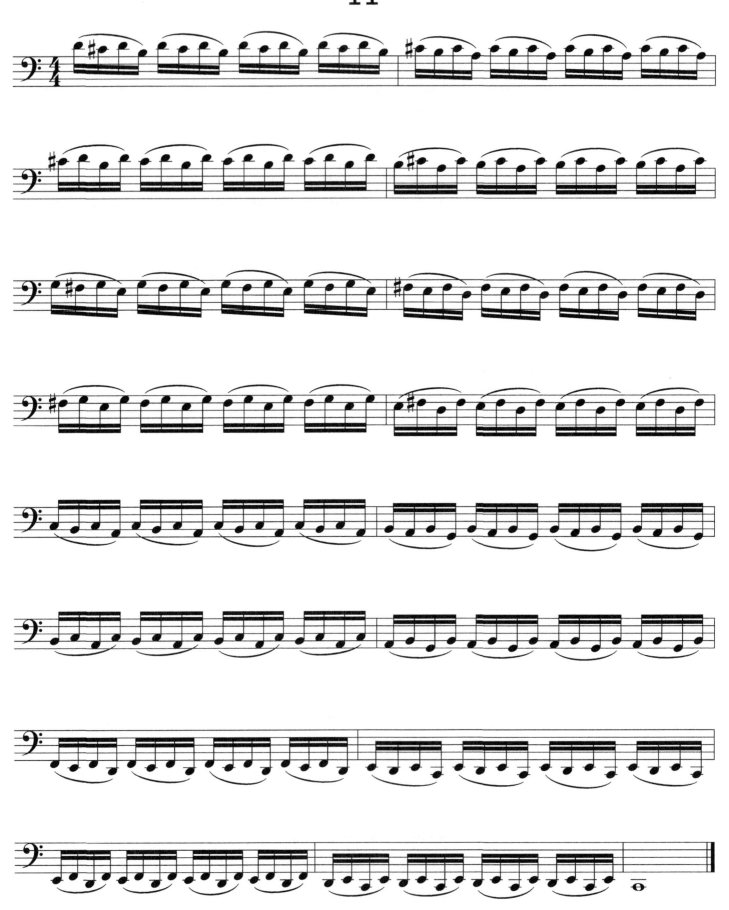

12

13

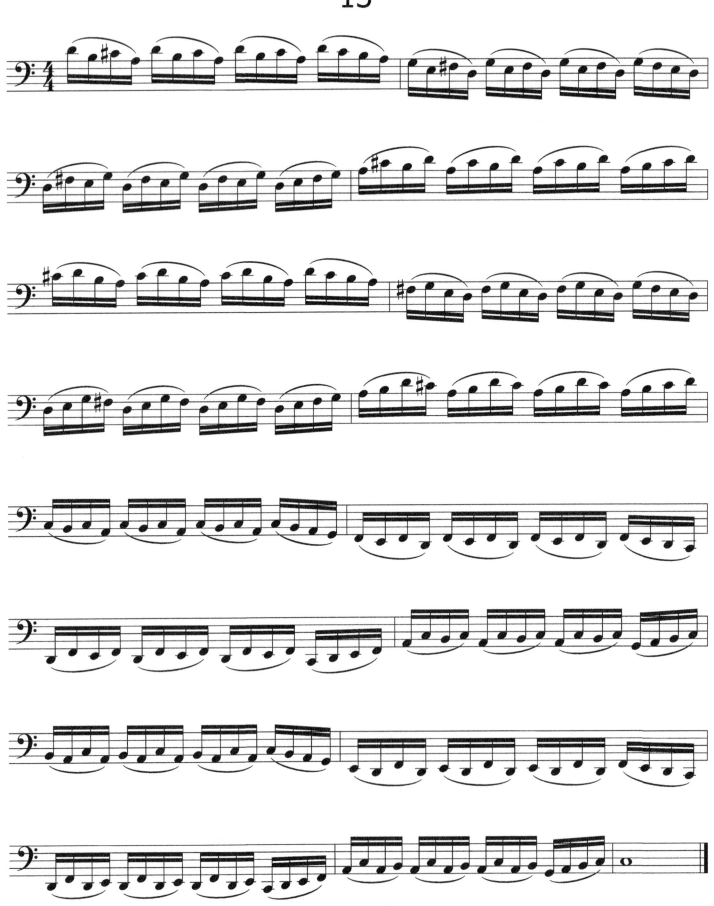

14

These two measures are played the same.

15

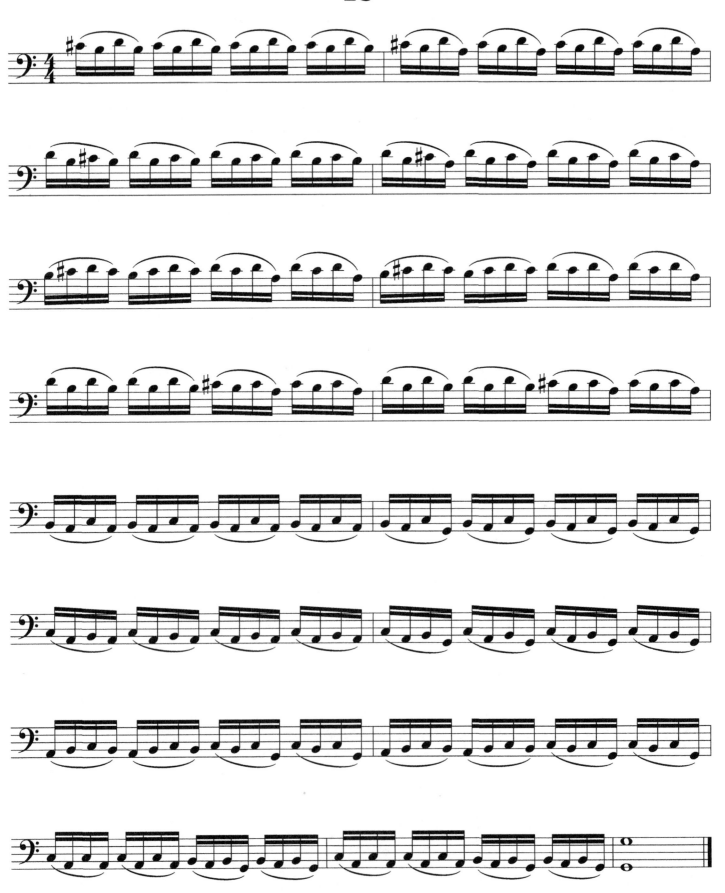

16

17

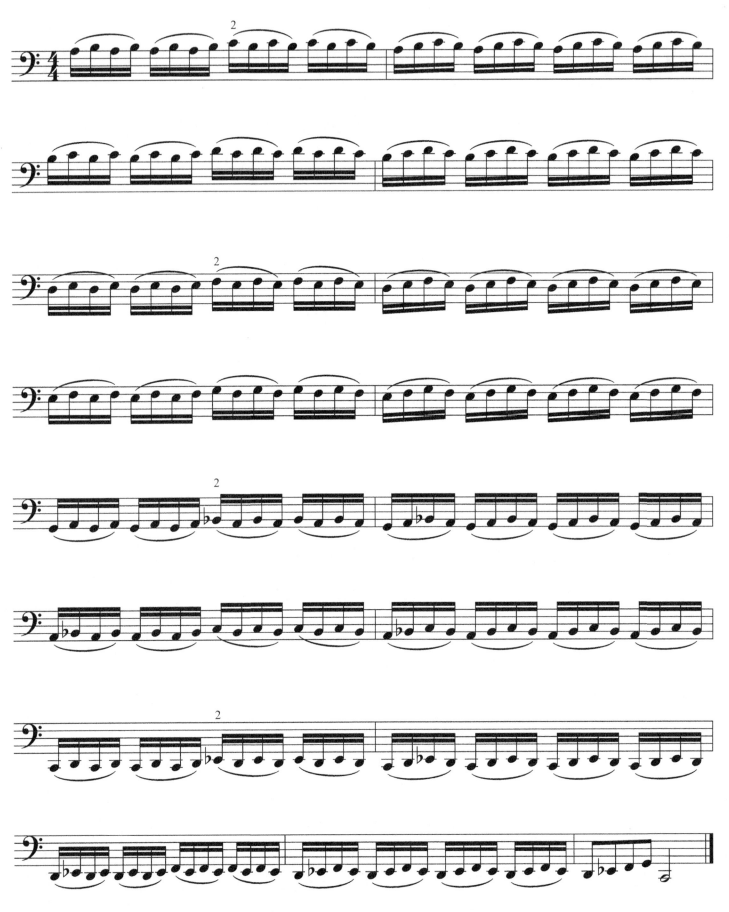

18

19

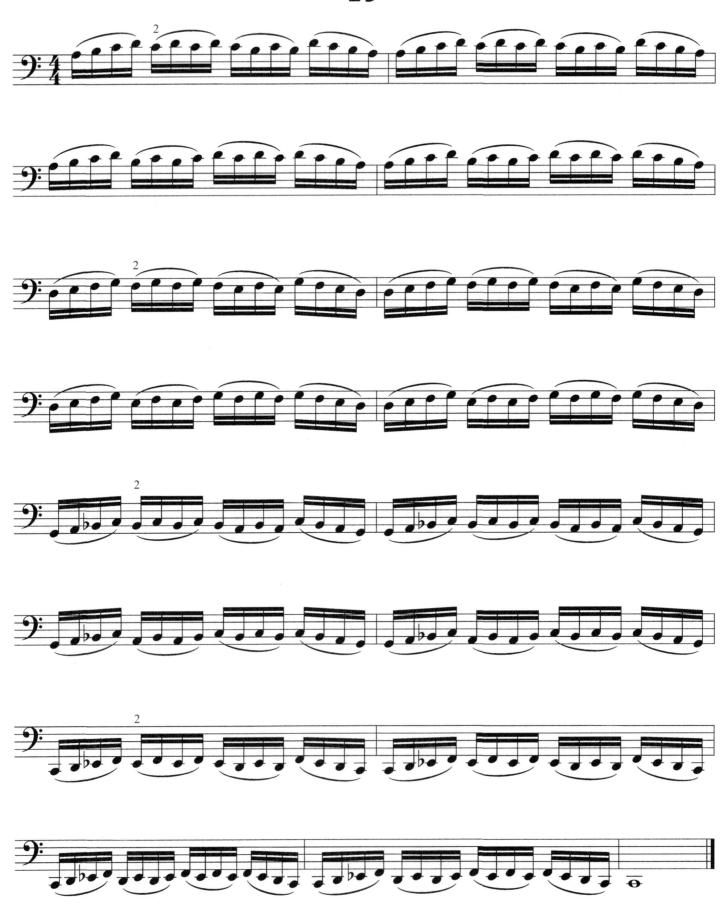

20

24

21

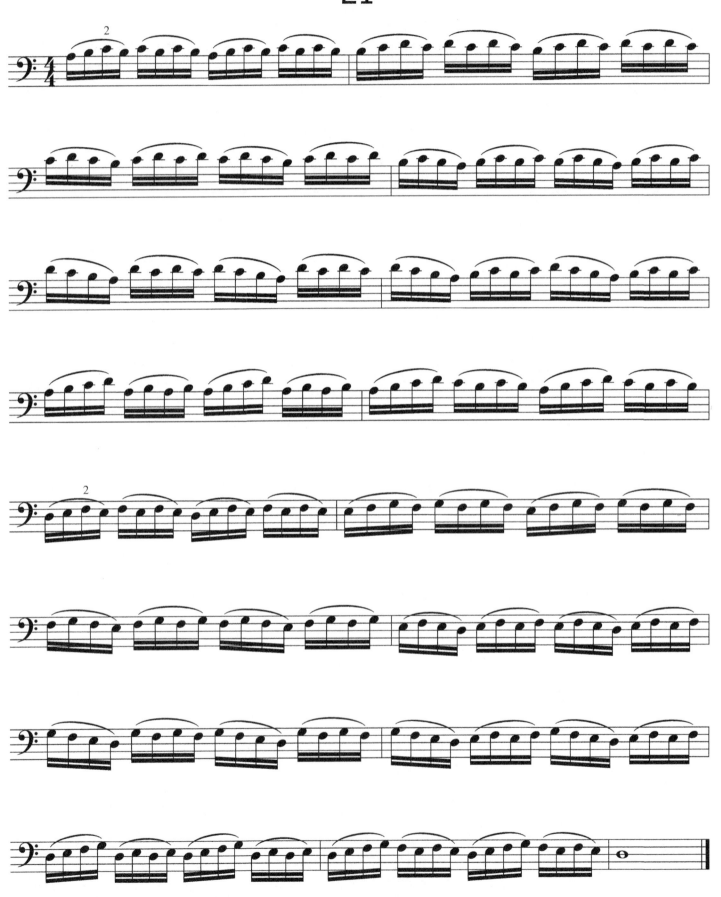

22

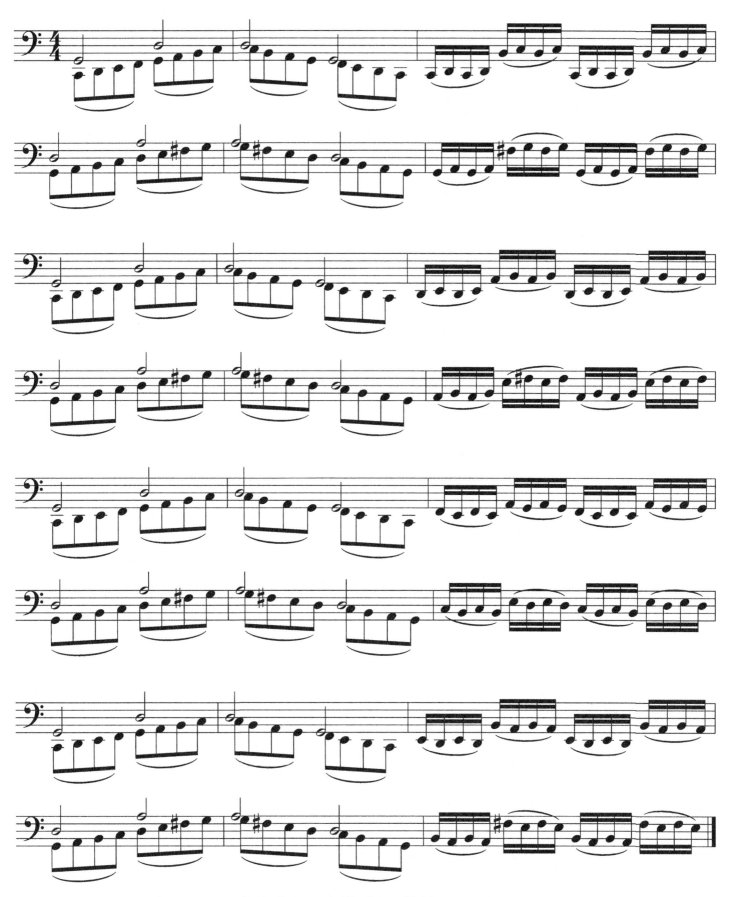

23

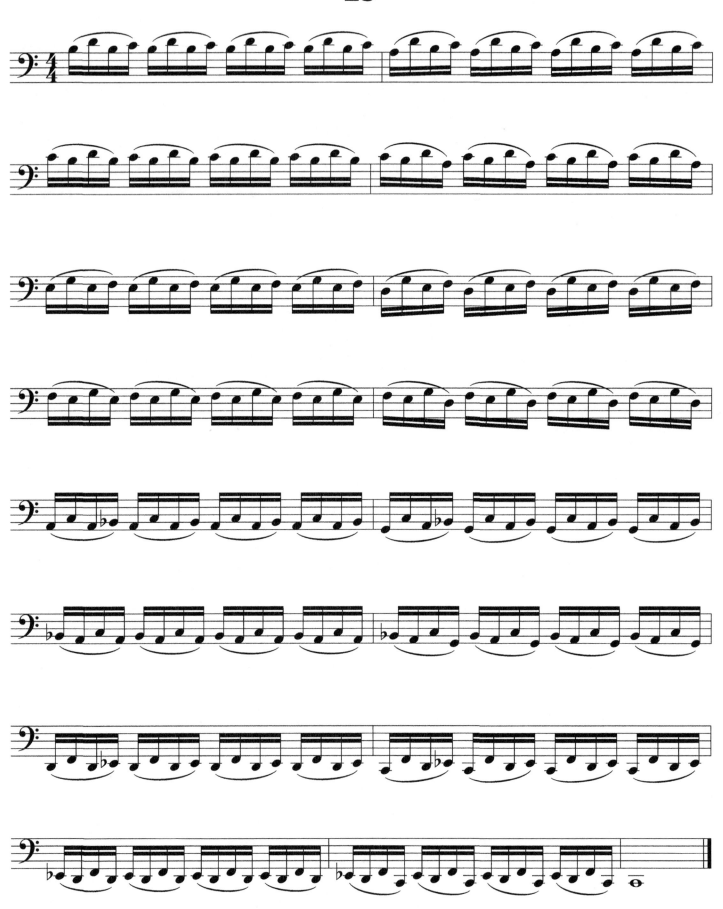

24

25

26

27

28

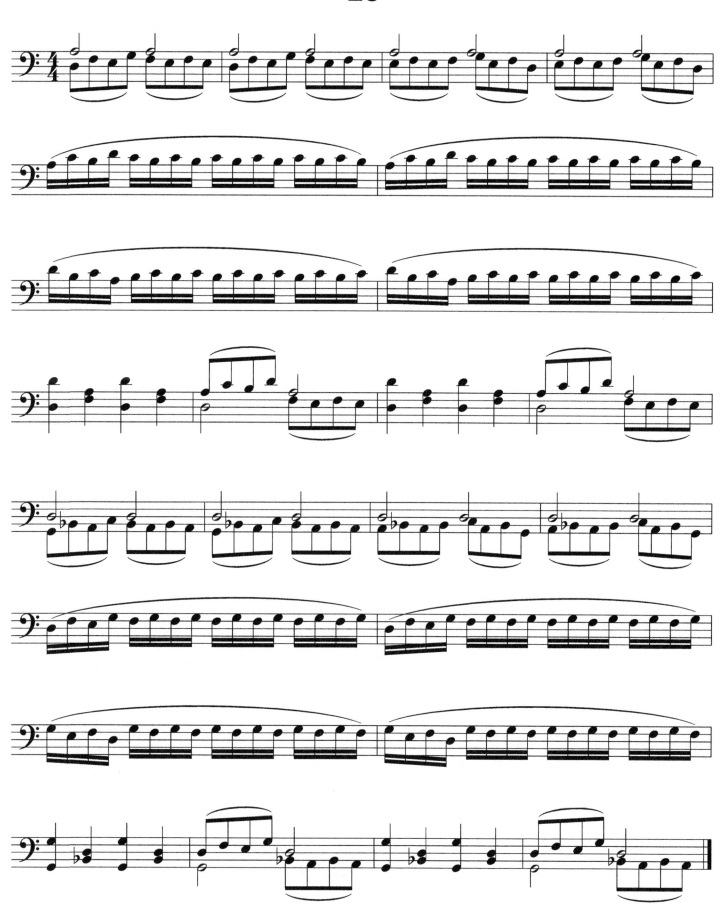

29

30

31

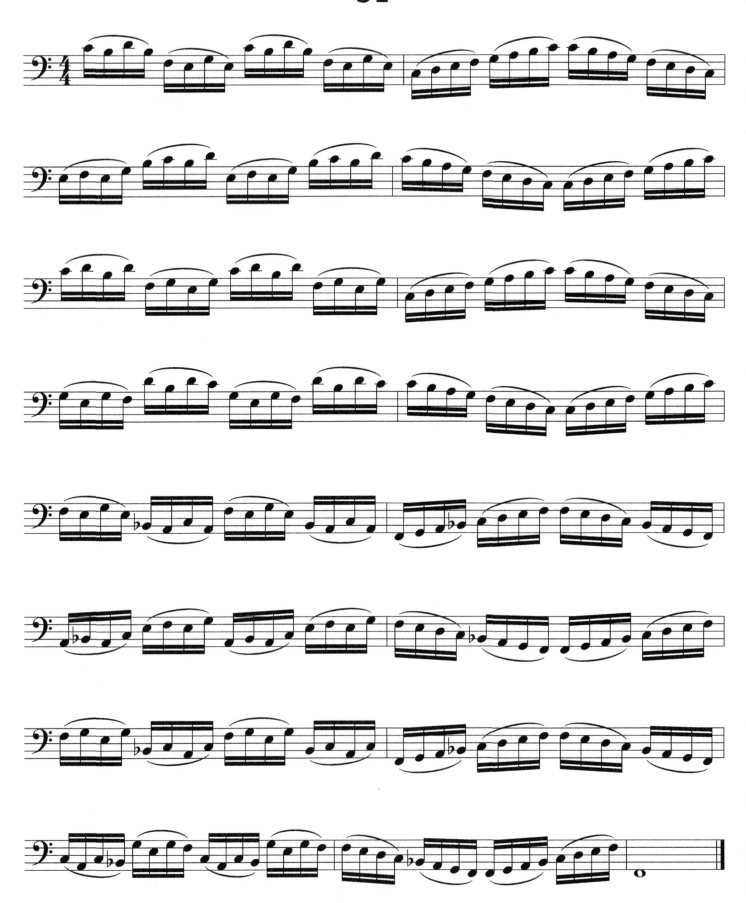

32

33

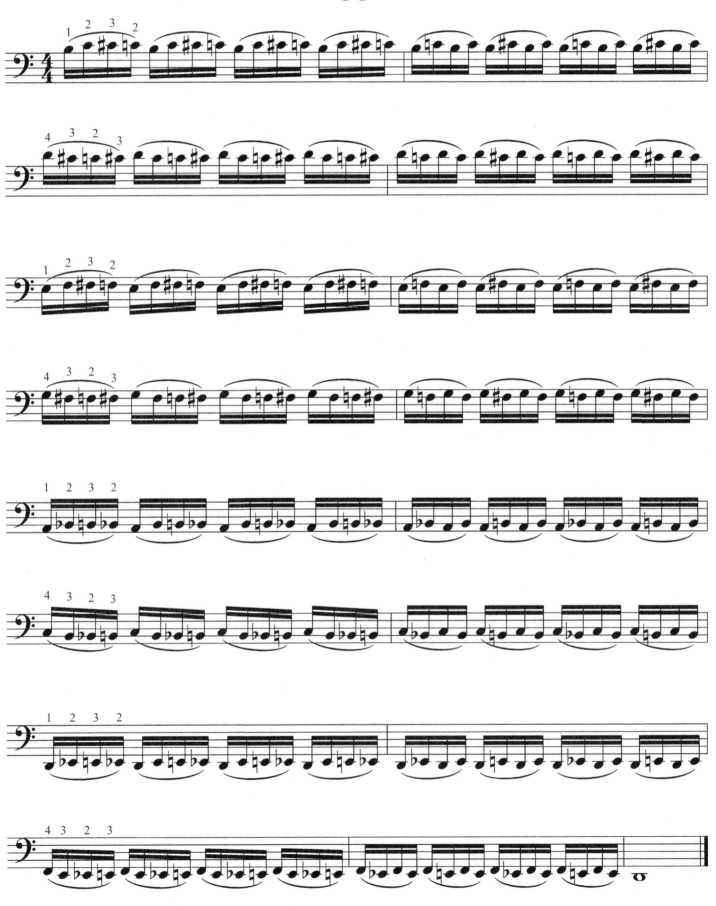

34

35

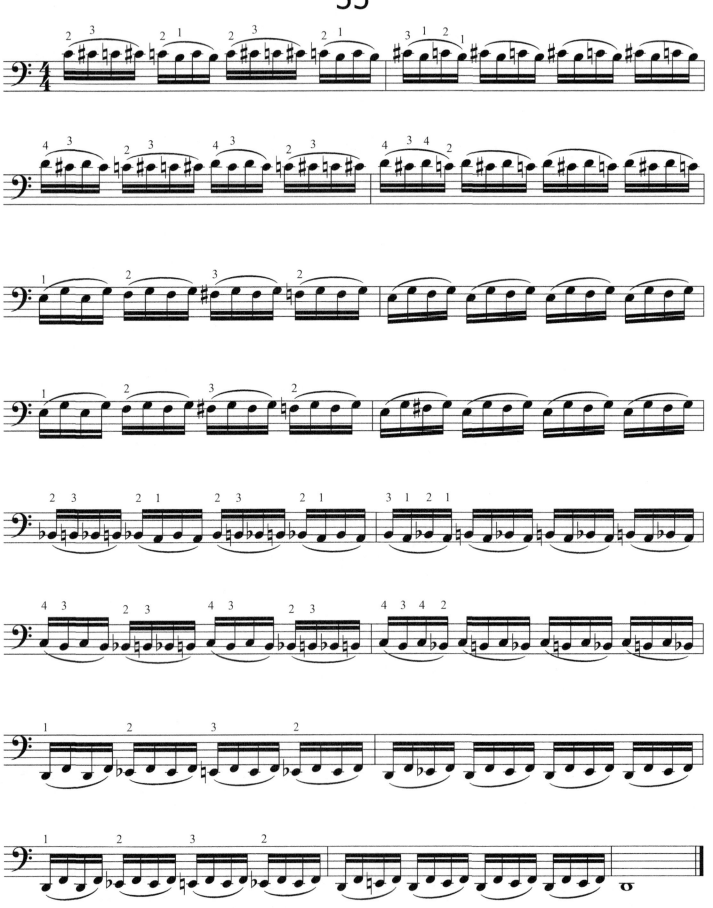

36

37

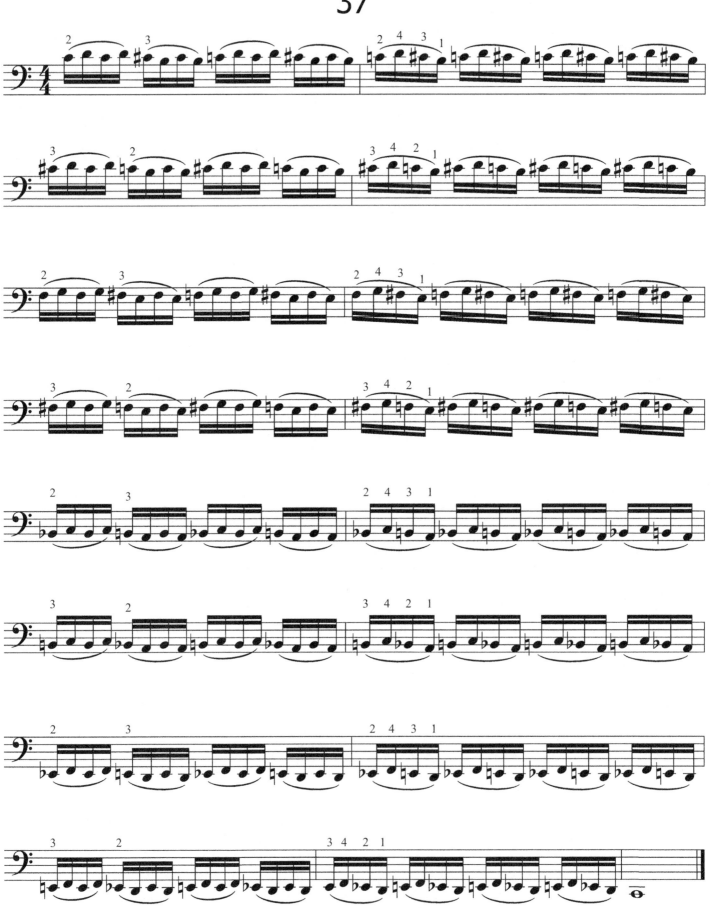

38

39

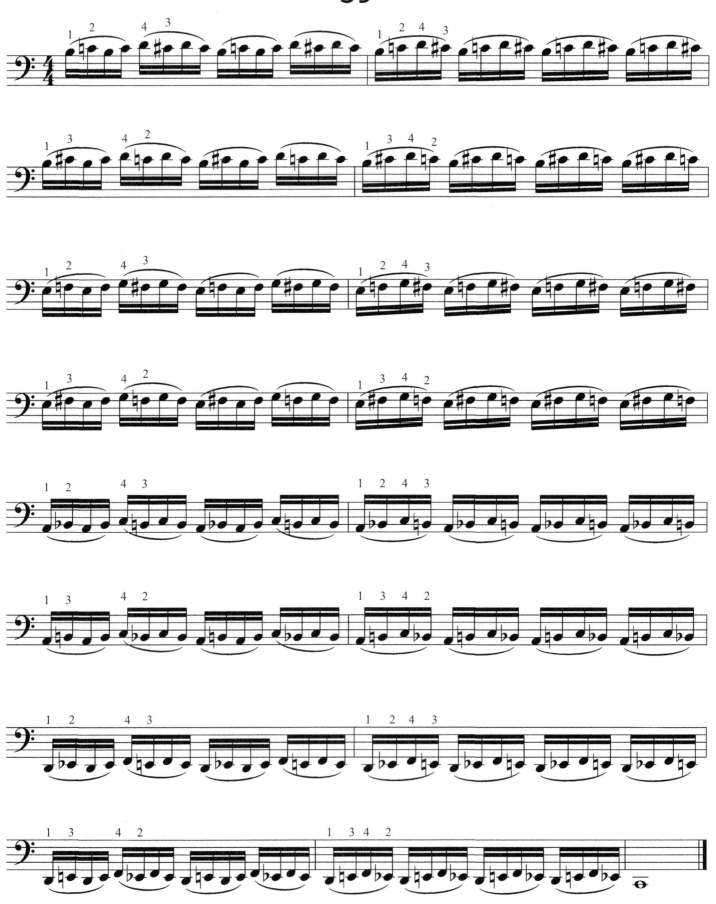

40

41

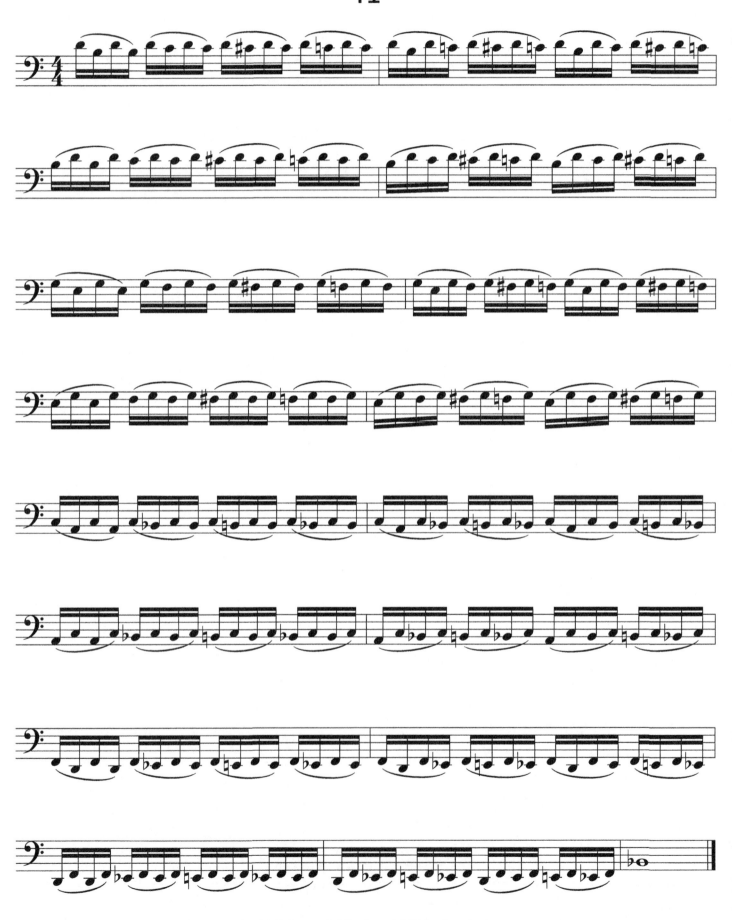

42

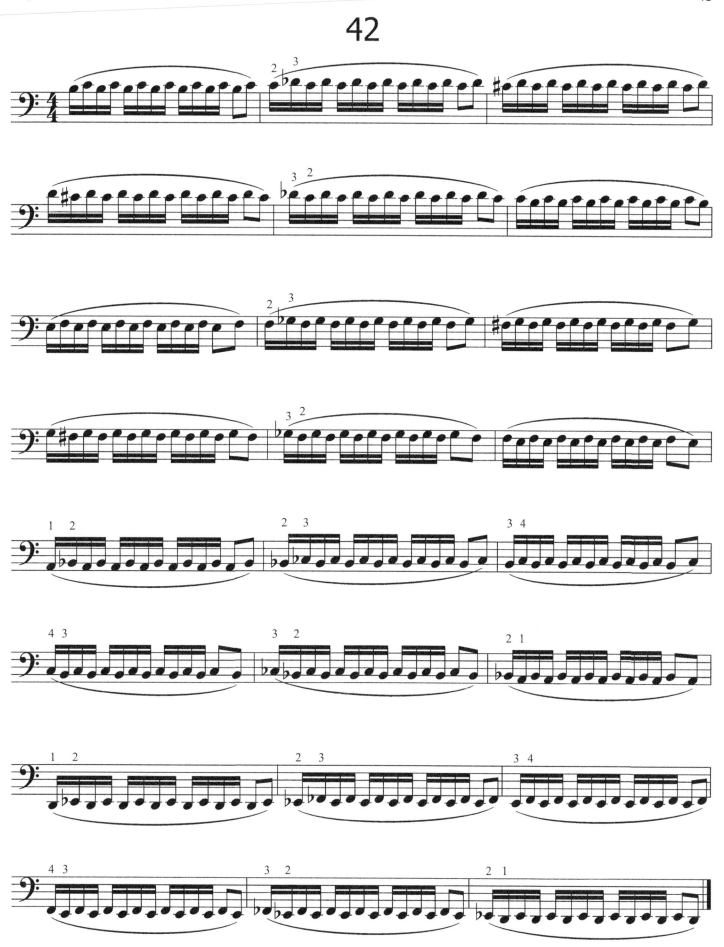

43

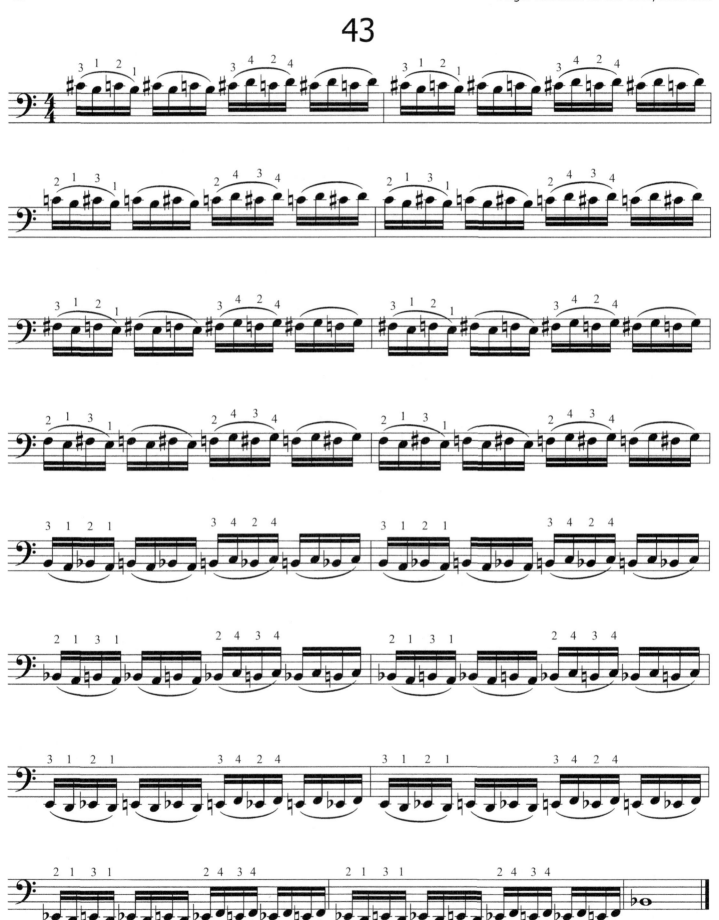

44

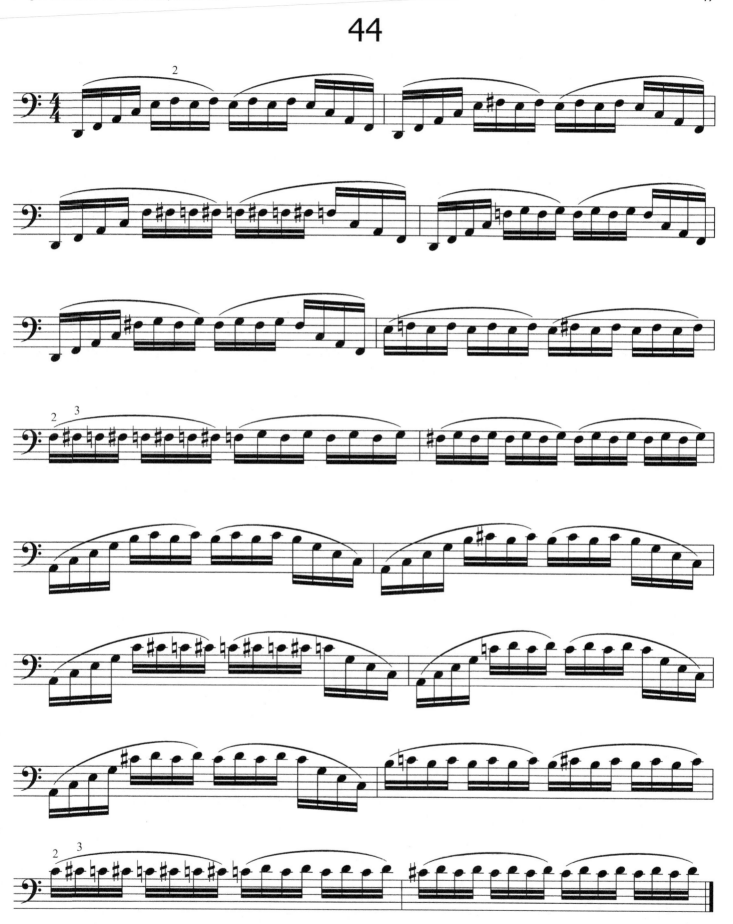

45

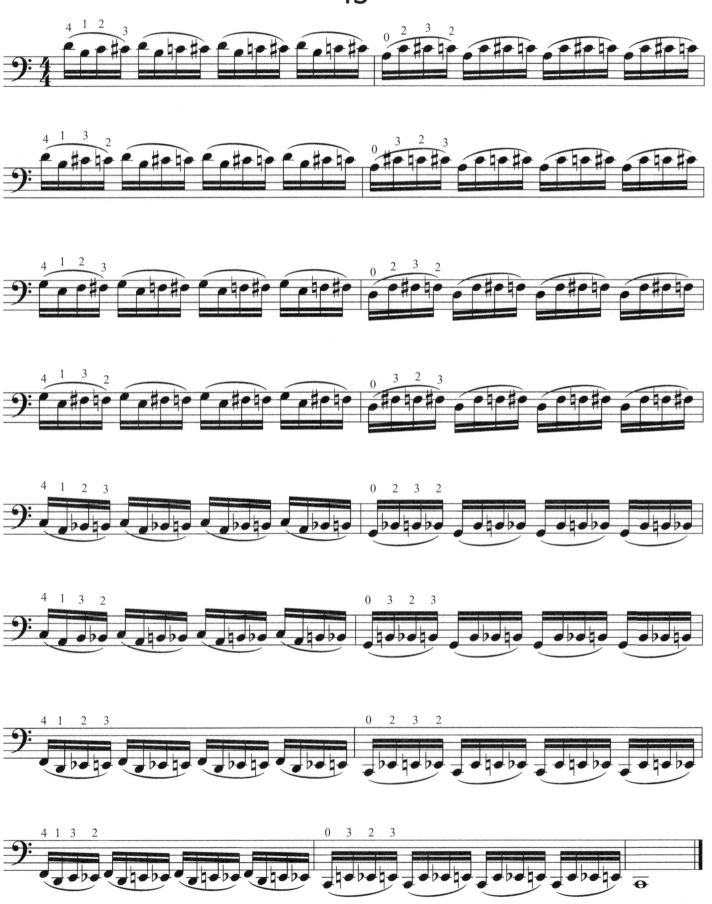

46

47

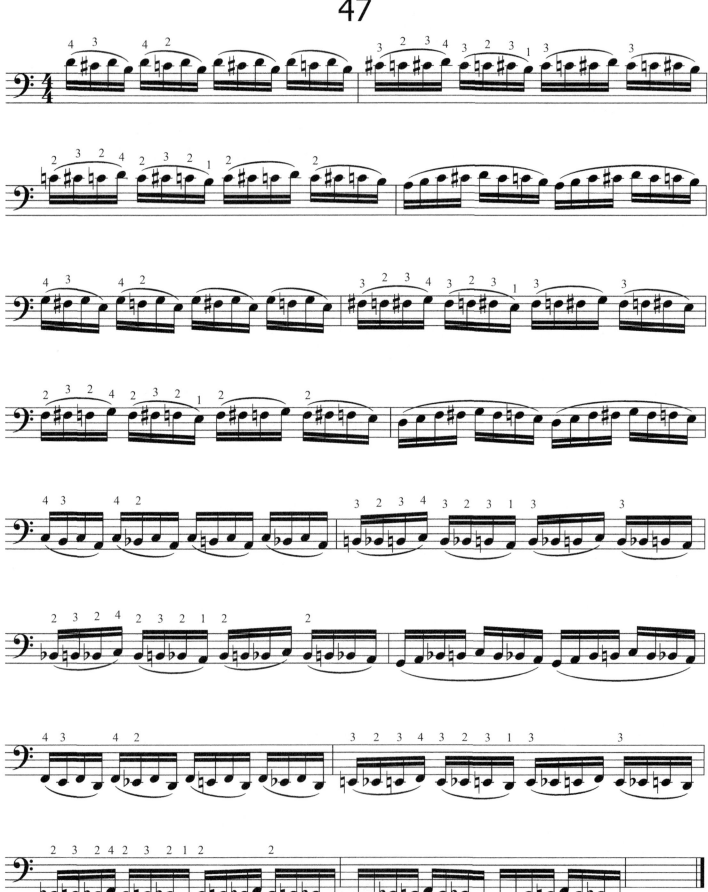

48

available from www.charveypublications.com

The Cello Etude System Part 0, Solo Book
CHP410 - etudes from the very beginning.

The Cello Etude System Part 0, Duet Book
CHP411 - etudes from the very beginning.

The Cello Etude System Part 1A, Solo Book CHP412
- curated, graded etudes in closed first position.

The Cello Etude System Part 1A, Duet Book CHP413
- curated, graded etudes in closed first position.

Printed in Great Britain
by Amazon

47154303R00031